Salads

JAN. 2002

WWP
JGP

Recipe	page	calories/portion	for staying slim	regional specialty	inexpensive	make ahead	sophisticated	easy	good for guests	fast
Asparagus Salad with Ham Mousse	6	210				●			●	
Shrimp, Green Bean, & Grapefruit Salad	6	330				●		◐		
Spinach Salad with Scallops	8	170	◐			●			●	
Arugula Salad with Air-Dried Beef	9	230				●	◐		●	◐
Melon & Cucumber Salad with Mint	10	200	◐			●		◐		
Artichoke Hearts with Prosciutto	10	400			●	●				
Frisée with Mango and Turkey Strips	12	360				●			●	
Mâche with Smoked Trout	13	300				●	◐		●	
Red Leaf Lettuce with Mushrooms & Bacon	14	280					◐		●	
Endive with Avocado and Smoked Salmon	14	240				●	◐			◐
Caesar Salad	18	500	●	◐				◐	●	
Salad Niçoise	19	350	●		●			◐		
Panzanella	20	390	●	◐	●			◐		
Farmer's Salad	20	430	●	◐	●			◐		◐
Noodle-Vegetable Salad	22	470	●			●				
Gado Gado	22	510	●						●	
Eggplant & Zucchini Salad	24	290	◐	●				◐		
Tabbouleh 24	24	270	●	●	◐					
Seafood Salad with Vegetables	26	330	●		●				●	
Herring Salad with Beets	27	870	●		●		◐			
Lamb Meatballs on Leaf Lettuce	30	670				●	◐		●	
Warm Vegetable Salad with Ginger	30	250	◐			●				
Steak Strips on Green Leaf Lettuce	32	300	◐					◐	●	◐
Cheese Salad with Garlicky Nuts	33	720				●	◐			
Shrimp on Snow Peas	34	450				●		◐	●	

Recipe

Recipe	page	calories/portion	for staying slim	regional specialty	inexpensive	make ahead	sophisticated	easy	good for guests	fast
Chicken Breast on Mixed Greens	34	570				●	●			●
Mâche with Chicken Livers	36	440				●	●	●		
Mushroom Salad with Peppers and Salami	37	440						●		●
Fresh Tuna on Radicchio	38	450						●		●
Oakleaf Lettuce with Warm Goat Cheese Toasts	38	640				●			●	●
Celery Root Salad with Mustard Dressing	42	450			●		●	●		
Tomato-Mozzarella Salad	42	340			●	●				●
Green Beans, Arugula, & Cherry Tomatoes	44	200	●						●	
Chicken Salad with Pineapple & Sprouts	45	550				●	●			
Cucumber Salad with Dill	46	190	●		●			●		●
Cucumber Salad with Strawberries	46	130	●				●	●		●
Cucumber Salad with Smoked Trout	47	250				●			●	●
Cucumber Salad with Sesame & Sprouts	47	170	●					●		●
Butter Lettuce with Radish Sprouts	48	140	●		●			●		●
German-Style Potato Salad	48	350			●	●		●		
Turkey Salad with Leeks and Oyster Mushrooms	52	220	●				●		●	
Green Pasta Salad with Parmesan Dressing	53	330				●	●	●	●	
Sausage Salad with Radishes	54	650		●	●			●	●	●
Hearty Lentil Salad	54	570			●	●			●	
Vegetable Salad with Mortadella	56	340						●	●	●
Egg Salad with Corn	56	310			●	●	●	●	●	
Rice Salad with Tuna and Tomatoes	58	350			●	●			●	
Iceberg Lettuce with Smoked Pork	59	300						●	●	●
Potato-Vegetable Salad	60	290			●	●		●	●	
Two-Bean Salad with Avocado Dressing	60	300				●			●	

Table

Elegant Appetizer Salads

The appetizer should always be in contrast to the main course. For example, a salad with fish or seafood goes well with a meat entrée; or, if fish is the main item, meat or poultry salads complement it well. In principle, the richer the main course, the lighter should be the appetizer. Appetizer salads look especially elegant and mouthwatering when served on large plates. If the salads contain fish or seafood, glass plates or glass bowls make an attractive presentation.

Bread is the Ideal Accompaniment

The simplest accompaniment is toasted and buttered sliced bread. Choose a high quality, freshly baked loaf, from a local bakery if possible. Heat the bread until it is hot and crusty, and serve it with fresh, creamy butter.

Homemade Garlic Bread

Another traditional accompaniment to salad is garlic bread. To prepare it, make deep cuts along the length of a baguette, about 1 inch apart, leaving the loaf in tact at the bottom. Stir finely minced fresh garlic to taste into softened butter, season with salt and pepper, and stir in some minced fresh Italian parsley (optional). Spread the butter generously into the slits in the bread, and wrap the loaf in aluminum foil. Place into a preheated 400°F oven until the butter is melted and the bread is warm and fragrant.

Bruschetta

For this Italian specialty, plunge a large, ripe tomato into boiling water to loosen the skin. With a paring knife, remove the skin and the stem. Cut the tomato in half and squeeze out the seeds. Cut the tomato flesh into small dice, and put into a bowl.

Wash, shake dry, and finely chop 1/2 bunch fresh basil, and add it to the bowl. Peel and mince 1 clove of garlic, and add it to the bowl. Stir in 1 tbs olive oil, and season with salt and pepper. Toast slices of Tuscan bread or baguette, place on a serving platter, and spoon the tomato mixture over the tops.

Pretty Shapes

Salad looks even more appealing when arranged decoratively. There are a few kitchen tools that can help.

Melon Baller: This tool cuts small balls from fruits or vegetables. It is especially useful for firm items, such as cucumbers, zucchini, melons, apples, and pears.

Spoons: Spoons work like a melon ballers to cut semi-soft items, like fruit. To use, dip soup spoons into hot water. Insert a soup spoon into the fruit to cut out a spoon-shaped portion. You can also use teaspoons to make several small spoonfuls of fruit to garnish the salad.

Notch Maker: This modified knife features a raised hole which, when run along the surface of a vegetable or fruit, strips off notches of the food item to give it a decorative edge.

Ribbed Vegetable Knife: This knife has an exaggerated serrated surface that creates a ribbed surface when run through a vegetable or fruit. This works especially well for carrots, zucchini, or cucumbers.

Zester: This tool's main purpose is to remove the peel of the citrus fruit in long, beautiful strips. The tool's special construction—a series of raised holes fastened to a long handle—allows you to remove strips of the colored part of the citrus peel (zest) without removing the bitter white substance (pith) that lies underneath it.

clockwise from bottom left: ribbed knife, notch maker, zester, melon baller

Working with Mangos

Peel the mango with a vegetable peeler. Cut triangular clefts into the fruit lengthwise all around the pit and remove wedges of the mango flesh.

Blanching Vegetables

To blanch vegetables, plunge them into boiling, salted water for a few minutes until tender-crisp. Drain the vegetables, then quickly plunge them into a bowl of ice water to lock in the intense, fresh color, and stop the cooking process.

Asparagus Salad with Ham Mousse

- make ahead
- good for guests

Serves 4:
8 oz cooked ham
1/2 cup crème fraîche
Salt & pepper to taste
Pinch of cayenne pepper
Fresh lemon juice to taste
1 lb white asparagus
1 lb green asparagus
3 tbs white wine vinegar
1 tsp Dijon-style mustard
1/4 cup canola oil
Handful of fresh Italian
   parsley leaves

Preparation time: 75 minutes
Per serving: 330 calories
17 g protein / 18 g fat / 6 g
carbohydrates

1 Remove the fat and rind from the ham, if necessary. Cut the ham into large pieces, and place them in a food processor or blender. Add the crème fraîche, and process until smooth. Transfer the mixture to a bowl, and season the mixture with salt, pepper, cayenne, and lemon juice. Cover the bowl, and refrigerate for 1 hour.

2 Meanwhile, bring a large amount of salted water to a boil. Carefully peel the white asparagus from top to bottom, and trim off the lower ends of the stalks. Wash the green asparagus, peel the lower third of the stalks, and trim off the ends. Cut the green and white asparagus in pieces about 1 1/4 inches long; set the asparagus tips aside.

3 Simmer the white asparagus in the water for 6 minutes. Add the green asparagus, and simmer for 10 more minutes. Add the tips for the last 5 minutes of cooking. Drain the asparagus through a sieve or colander.

4 In a bowl, mix the vinegar with salt and the mustard, until the salt is dissolved. While whisking, add the canola oil in a slow stream to make a dressing.

5 Put the asparagus in a bowl, and pour the dressing over it. Rinse the parsley, add to the bowl, and mix well. Let the salad stand for 15 minutes.

6 With a tablespoon, cut out spoonfuls of the ham mousse, and arrange them on 4 plates. Arrange the asparagus salad on top of the mousse.

Shrimp, Green Bean, & Grapefruit Salad

- easy
- sophisticated

Serves 4:
Salt to taste
8 oz thin green beans
2 pink grapefruits
1 head romaine lettuce
2 shallots
1/4 cup balsamic vinegar
Pepper to taste
Pinch of cayenne pepper
5 tbs peanut oil
6 oz cooked and peeled
, shrimp

Preparation time: 30 minutes
Per serving: 210 calories
10 g protein / 11 g fat / 15 g
carbohydrates

1 Bring a large pot of salted water to a boil. Wash the beans, cut off the ends, and remove the strings if necessary. Cook the beans in the water until tender-crisp, about 5-8 minutes. Drain the beans, immediately plunge them into ice water, and drain well.

2 With a long, sharp knife, cut off the peel and inner white pith of the grapefruits to expose the fruit. Run the knife alongside each of the fruit's membranes to release the grapefruit segments. Remove the grapefruit seeds, and cut the segments into pieces.

3 Trim the romaine lettuce, and cut it into finger-width strips. Wash and dry the lettuce.

4 Peel and finely chop the shallots. In a small bowl, mix the vinegar with the salt, pepper, and cayenne pepper. While whisking, add the peanut oil in a slow stream to make a dressing, then stir in the shallots.

5 In a large bowl, gently toss the beans, grapefruit pieces, and romaine lettuce with the salad dressing to taste, and distribute the salad on 4 plates. Place the shrimp on top and drizzle with the remaining dressing.

Serving suggestions:
Serve with buttered sliced crusty bread and glasses of Prosecco (Italian Sparkling Wine).

below: Asparagus Salad
with Ham Mousse
above: Shrimp, Green
Bean, & Grapefruit Salad

Spinach Salad with Scallops

- for staying slim
- good for guests

Serves 4:
8 oz fresh spinach
1 shallot
3 tbs sherry vinegar
3 tbs toasted sesame oil
1 tbs soy sauce
Salt & pepper to taste
6 oz cherry tomatoes
8 oz sea scallops, side
  muscle removed
2 tbs butter

Preparation time: 35 minutes
Per serving: 170 calories
8 g protein / 13 g fat / 5 g
carbohydrates

1 Sort through the spinach and remove the stems. Wash the spinach thoroughly several times and dry it. Peel and finely chop the shallot.

2 In a large bowl, whisk together the sherry vinegar, oil, soy sauce, salt, and pepper to make a dressing.

3 Wash the tomatoes, cut them in half, and place them in the bowl along with the spinach and the shallot. Add salad dressing to taste and toss the ingredients well. Divide the salad among 4 serving plates.

4 Rinse the scallops with cold water and pat dry. In a skillet, melt the butter over medium-high heat. Add the scallops and sear for 3 minutes on each side. Season with salt and pepper and cool slightly. Arrange the scallops over the spinach salad.

Serving suggestions:
Serve with a buttered, toasted baguette, and perhaps a dry white wine or Champagne.

Arugula Salad with Air-Dried Beef

● sophisticated
◐ easy

Serves 4:
2 bunches arugula
8 oz cherry tomatoes
2 tbs sherry vinegar
5 tbs olive oil
Salt & pepper to taste
Pinch of sugar
1 bunch fresh Italian
   parsley
2 cloves garlic
1 egg
8 thin slices baguette
6 oz thinly sliced Swiss
   Bundnerfleisch

Preparation time: 25 minutes
Per serving : 230 calories / 12 g
protein / 15 g fat / 13 g
carbohydrates

1 Sort the arugula, and cut off any coarse stems. Wash and dry the arugula. Wash the tomatoes, cut them in half, and arrange them on 4 plates with the arugula.

2 In a small bowl, whisk together the vinegar, 3 tbs of the olive oil, salt, pepper, and sugar to make a dressing. Drizzle it over the salad.

3 Wash and shake dry the parsley, pick off the leaves, and finely chop them. Place the parsley on a plate. Peel and mince the garlic, and mix it with the parsley. In a shallow dish, beat the egg and season with salt and pepper.

4 Dip the baguette slices into the egg, coating both sides, then turn them in the parsley mixture. In a skillet, heat the remaining 2 tbs olive oil over medium heat. Add the coated bread slices and fry until golden brown on both sides.

5 Roll up the meat slices and arrange them on top of the salad. Serve with the fried bread slices.

Tip! Look for Swiss Bundnerfleisch in a specialty foods store. Or, substitute your favorite type of cured meat or fish.

Melon & Cucumber Salad with Mint

◐ easy
● for staying slim

Serves 4:
1 cucumber
1 charentais melon or
  cantaloupe (about
  1 1/4 lb)
1 bunch fresh mint
1 small bunch fresh Italian
  parsley
5 tbs fresh lemon juice
Pinch of sugar
Salt & pepper to taste
5 tbs sunflower oil
6 oz cooked and peeled
  shrimp

Preparation time: 30 minutes
Per serving: 200 calories / 10 g
protein / 13 g fat / 12 g
carbohydrates

1 Peel the cucumber, cut
it in half crosswise, then
quarter it lengthwise.
Remove the seeds with a
spoon, and cut the flesh
into pieces about 1/3-
inch long. Cut the melon
into eighths, remove the
seeds, loosen the fruit
from the rind, and cut the
fruit into bite-sized
pieces. Put the melon and
cucumber in a large bowl.

2 Wash and shake dry
the mint and parsley.
Remove the herb leaves
from the stems, coarsely
chop the leaves, and add

them to the bowl.

3 In a small bowl, stir
together the lemon juice,
sugar, salt, pepper, and oil
to make a dressing, and
pour over the salad
ingredients. Add the
shrimp, toss everything
well, and let the salad
stand for 10 minutes.

Artichoke Hearts with Prosciutto

● sophisticated
● make ahead

Serves 4:
2 cans artichoke hearts
  (13.75 oz cans)
1 small onion
1 clove garlic
1 tbs olive oil
Salt & pepper to taste
Dash of cayenne pepper
Dash of sugar
1 sprig fresh thyme
1 cup dry white wine (or
  chicken stock)
1/4 cup white wine
  vinegar
1 red bell pepper
1 yellow bell pepper
6 oz sliced prosciutto (not
  too thin)
Lettuce leaves for serving

Preparation time: 30 minutes
Per serving: 400 calories / 11 g
protein / 18 g fat / 21 g
carbohydrates

1 Drain the artichoke
hearts and cut them into
halves or quarters,
depending on size. Put
the artichoke hearts in
a bowl.

2 Peel and finely chop
the onion and garlic. In a
small skillet, heat the oil
over medium heat. Add
the onion and sauté until
translucent. Add the
garlic and sauté briefly.
Season with salt, pepper,
cayenne pepper, and
sugar; add the thyme
sprig. Add the white wine
and 2 tbs of the white
wine vinegar, and bring to
a boil briefly. Pour the hot
mixture over the
artichokes, and let them
cool in a bowl.

3 Meanwhile, wash and
trim the red and yellow
peppers. Cut them first
into narrow strips, then
dice them very small. Cut
the prosciutto into
narrow strips.

4 With a slotted spoon,
lift the artichokes from
the marinade, and put
them in a large bowl
along with the diced
peppers and strips of
the prosciutto.

5 Transfer 3 tbs of the
artichoke marinade to a
small bowl. Whisk in the
remaining 2 tbs vinegar,
season with salt and
pepper, and pour it over

the salad ingredients. Toss everything well and refrigerate until ready to serve. Line 4 serving plates with the lettuce leaves and distribute the salad on top.

Serving suggestions: Serve with sliced bread and dry sherry.

Tip! To save time, use marinated artichoke hearts from a jar and omit the initial marinating step and ingredients.

below: Artichoke Hearts with Prosciutto
above: Melon & Cucumber Salad with Mint

Frisée with Mango and Turkey Strips

● good for guests
● sophisticated

Serves 4:
1 lb boneless turkey breast
5 tbs soybean oil
Salt & pepper to taste
2 tbs sesame seeds
1 small head frisée lettuce (about 8 oz)
1 mango
2 tbs crème fraîche
1/2 tsp curry powder
4–5 tbs fresh lemon juice
1 tsp honey

Preparation time: 40 minutes
Per serving: 360 calories
25 g protein / 24 g fat / 11 g carbohydrates

1 Cut the turkey into 1/3-inch-wide strips. In a skillet, heat 2 tbs of the oil over medium heat. Add the turkey strips and sauté until cooked through, about 5 minutes. Season the meat with salt and pepper, and remove it from the pan. Add the sesame seeds to the pan and sauté briefly until light brown; set aside.

2 Trim the frisée, tear it apart, wash, and dry.

3 Peel the mango and cut the fruit from the pit (see p 5). In a food processor or blender, puree 1/3 of the fruit with the crème fraîche, seasoning with salt, pepper, the curry powder, and 2 tbs of the lemon juice. Cut the rest of the mango into small dice.

4 In a large bowl, whisk 2 tbs of the lemon juice with the remaining 3 tbs oil, the honey, salt, and pepper to make a dressing; add more lemon to taste. Add the frisée, toss to coat well with the dressing, and arrange it on 4 plates. Distribute the turkey strips over the frisée, and top with a dollop of mango puree. Sprinkle with the diced mango and the toasted sesame seeds.

Mâche with Smoked Trout

● sophisticated
◐ easy

Serves 4:
8 oz mâche (lamb's
  lettuce)
2 carrots
3 shallots
2 tbs herbal vinegar
Pinch of Dijon-style
  mustard
Salt & pepper to taste
3 tbs walnut oil
1 bunch fresh chives
2 tbs pine nuts
1 lb smoked trout filets

Preparation time: 30 minutes
Per serving: 300 calories
23 g protein / 19 g fat / 9 g
carbohydrates

1 Trim, wash, and dry the lettuce. Peel and grate the carrots. Peel and finely chop the shallots.

2 In a large bowl, stir together the vinegar, mustard, salt, and pepper. While whisking, add the oil in a thin stream to make a dressing. Wash, shake dry, and mince the chives. Stir half of the chives, and the shallots, into the dressing.

3 In a dry nonstick skillet, toast the pine nuts until golden brown.

4 Toss the mâche and the carrots in the salad dressing, and mix in the pine nuts. Distribute the salad among 4 plates.

5 Cut the trout filets into bite-sized pieces and arrange them on the salad. Sprinkle the remaining chives on top.

Red Leaf Lettuce with Mushrooms and Bacon

● good for guests
● easy

Serves 4:
1 head red leaf lettuce
3 tbs sherry vinegar
5 tbs walnut oil
Salt & pepper to taste
4 oz bacon
4 cloves garlic
8 oz oyster mushrooms

Preparation time: 30 minutes
Per serving: 280 calories
9 g protein / 26 g fat / 4 g
carbohydrates

1 Wash the lettuce, tear larger leaves into pieces, and dry well. In a large bowl, whisk together the sherry vinegar, walnut oil, salt, and pepper to make a dressing.

2 Dice the bacon small. Peel the garlic and cut it into thin slices. If necessary, trim any hard ends off the oyster mushrooms, and cut the mushrooms into strips.

3 Heat a skillet over medium heat, add the bacon, and sauté until the fat is melted. Add the mushrooms and garlic, and sauté until the bacon is slightly crisp, about 5-7 minutes (stir constantly to prevent the garlic from burning).

4 Add the lettuce to the bowl with the dressing and toss to coat well. Distribute the salad on 4 plates. Season the mushrooms with salt and pepper, divide them among the plates, and serve while the mushrooms are still warm.

Variation
For variety, choose a mixture of lettuces, such as radicchio, arugula, and frisée.

Endive with Avocado and Smoked Salmon

○ fast
● sophisticated

Serves 4:
1 lb Belgian endive
1/4 cup fresh lemon juice
5 tbs extra-virgin olive oil
Pinch of sugar
Salt & pepper to taste
1 ripe avocado
8 oz smoked salmon, thinly sliced

Preparation time: 20 minutes
Per serving: 240 calories / 12 g
protein / 18 g fat / 9 g
carbohydrates

1 Trim the Belgian endive, tear off the individual leaves, and cut out the bitter core. Wash and dry the endive.

2 In a large bowl, whisk together 2 tbs of the lemon juice, the oil, sugar, salt, and pepper to make a dressing.

3 Peel the avocado, cut it in half lengthwise, and remove the pit. Cut the avocado into slices, and drizzle the slices with the remaining 2 tbs lemon juice. Season lightly with salt and pepper.

4 Put the endive in the bowl and toss to coat with the dressing. Distribute the endive leaves on 4 plates, forming star shapes. Drizzle the leaves with the dressing remaining in the bowl. Roll up the smoked salmon slices and arrange them, along with the avocado, on top of the endive.

Variation
For the smoked salmon, substitute pieces of smoked trout or sliced grilled chicken breast.

below: Endive with Avocado and Smoked Salmon
above: Read Leaf Lettuce with Mushrooms and Bacon

Inter-national Salads

Every country has its own specialties created from local ingredients and customs. For example, in the Mediterranean region vegetables, olives, tomatoes, garlic, and herbs are popular in salads. In Asia, Chinese noodles, ginger, sesame oil, and fruits are common ingredients. In the Middle East, salads often consist of grains like couscous and bulgur, and are often strongly spiced with such things as fresh mint, saffron, cumin, and fresh lemon juice. Avocados, corn, beans, and chiles dominate salads from Mexico and other South-American countries.

Other dishes become associated with a country because of their popularity, not necessarily their origin. Caesar salad is a good example. Though a standard on U.S. restaurant menus, most people believe the Caesar to be an Italian invention, though it was actually invented in Tijuana.

Global Salad Staples

• Couscous is steam-treated hard-wheat granules, similar to tiny pasta beads. Couscous is a common ingredient in North-African salads. Look for couscous in well-stocked supermarkets and in health food stores.

• Glass noodles, also called cellophane noodles, are thin, Asian noodles made from rice flour. After soaking in boiling water, they become nearly transparent, which explains how they got their name. Somewhat bland in flavor, glass noodles are a good base for salads that have a lot spices and other bold-tasting flavorings.

• Fresh ginger—
Botanically a rhizome, though often considered a root, fresh ginger has a distinct intense, flavor and is common in Asian-style salads. It's best purchased fresh, in quantities just large enough for the recipes. Fresh ginger should be peeled and chopped just before using.

• Toasted sesame oil—sometimes called Asian sesame oil—has a wonderful, nutty flavor, and is used in small amounts for seasoning. Look for it in Asian foods stores and well-stocked supermarkets.

• Bean sprouts can be found in the fresh produce section of the supermarket. Though mung bean sprouts are the most widely available, look for fresh soybean sprouts, which are more flavorful and nutritious. The sprouts should be as white as possible. For best results, plunge the bean sprouts in boiling water for a few seconds, then refresh them in ice water.

• Anchovy fillets add punch and sophistication to many types of Mediterranean-style salads and salad dressings. Look for anchovy fillets packed in small, flat cans. Anchovies can be quite salty, so you may wish to rinse them with cold water, then pat dry, just before using.

About Garnishing

Here a few garnishing tips so that the eyes have something to feast on as well as the mouth.

• Parmesan cheese looks pretty when peeled into thin strips with a vegetable peeler, then sprinkled on the salad.

• Chile blossoms are very decorative and easy to make: With a small sharp knife, make several small cuts down the length of the chile from the stem to the tip. Place the chile in a bowl of ice water for 30 minutes; the ends will curl up to resemble a blossom.

• Like chiles, green onions can also be cut to resemble blossoms: Cut off the root end of an onion, then cut the onion into a 4-inch piece, starting from the white part (reserve the green part for another use). With a small sharp knife, make several tiny cuts starting from where the root end used to be. Place the onion in a bowl of ice water for 30 minutes; the ends will curl up to resemble a blossom.

• Instead of searching for the expensive thin green beans, *haricots verts*, purchase regular, wide green beans and cut them lengthwise into thin strips.

• When using shrimp in a salad, purchase those with the tail fin in tact. Even if using peeled shrimp in your salad, the shrimp tail adds a little flair to the presentation.

left: cooked shrimp with tail fins in tact
right: clockwise from lower left—sheep's cheese, anchovy filets, olives, herring filets, bottled salad dressing from the US, olive oil, bulgur wheat, glass noodles

Caesar Salad

- good for guests
- specialty from America

Serves 4:

1 head romaine lettuce
2 cloves garlic
2 anchovy fillets (optional)
2 very fresh egg yolks
1/2 cup olive oil
2–3 tbs fresh lemon juice
2 oz Parmesan cheese,
　freshly grated
Salt & pepper to taste
3 slices sandwich bread
3 tbs butter

Preparation time: 30 minutes
Per serving: 500 calories
12 g protein / 44 g fat / 15 g
carbohydrates

1 Trim, wash, and dry the lettuce. Tear large leaves into pieces.

2 Peel and mince the garlic. Chop the anchovy fillets finely (if using). Place the egg yolks in a bowl. While mixing with an electric mixer, slowly add the oil in a thin stream until a thick, creamy mixture forms. Stir in the lemon juice. Stir in 1/2 of the garlic, the anchovy (if using), and 1/2 of the Parmesan cheese, and season with salt and pepper.

3 Put the lettuce in a large bowl. Add the dressing and toss well. Arrange the salad on 4 serving plates.

4 Remove the crusts from the bread, and cut into small dice. In a skillet, heat the butter over medium heat. Add the bread cubes and sauté until golden brown on all sides. Add the remaining garlic and sauté briefly. Sprinkle the bread cubes and remaining Parmesan over the salad and serve.

Tip! For a heartier meal—perfect for a luncheon—add strips of grilled chicken breast, steak, salmon, or peeled shrimp to the salad.

Note:
If you are concerned about the safety of the raw eggs in your area, substitute 1/4 cup frozen pasteurized egg yolks for the fresh egg yolks.

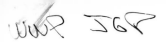

Salad Niçoise

● make ahead
● specialty from France

Serves 4:
3 eggs
Salt to taste
6 oz thin green beans
8 oz tomatoes
1 small head butter lettuce
1 can water-packed tuna
(6 oz)
5 anchovy fillets
1/2 cucumber
1/4 cup white wine vinegar
1 tsp Dijon-style mustard
Pepper to taste
6 tbs olive oil
4 oz black olives, pitted

Preparation time: 30 minutes
Per serving: 350 calories
17 g protein / 27 g fat / 11 g
carbohydrates

1 Boil the eggs for about 10 minutes, until the yolks are cooked hard. Plunge the eggs into ice water, let them stand for a few minutes, then peel and rinse.

2 Meanwhile bring a large pot of salted water to a boil. Trim the beans, remove the strings, and cut them into pieces about 1-inch long. Cook the beans in the water for 10 minutes, until tender-crisp. Drain the beans, plunge them into ice water, and drain again.

3 Wash the tomatoes, remove the stems, and cut the tomatoes into quarters or eighths. Trim, wash, and dry the lettuce. Tear the lettuce into bite-sized pieces. Drain the tuna and break it into pieces. Rinse the anchovies with cold water, pat dry, and cut them in half. Wash the cucumber and cut it into thin slices.

4 In a small bowl, whisk together the white wine vinegar, mustard, salt, pepper, and olive oil to make a dressing.

5 Place the lettuce in a large bowl. Drizzle with a small amount of the dressing, and toss well. Transfer the salad to a serving platter, or divide it among 4 plates. Add the beans, tomatoes, cucumber, tuna, anchovies, and olives to the large bowl, drizzle with the remaining dressing, and gently toss to coat the ingredients. Arrange the ingredients on top of the lettuce. Cut the eggs into quarters, and arrange on the salad.

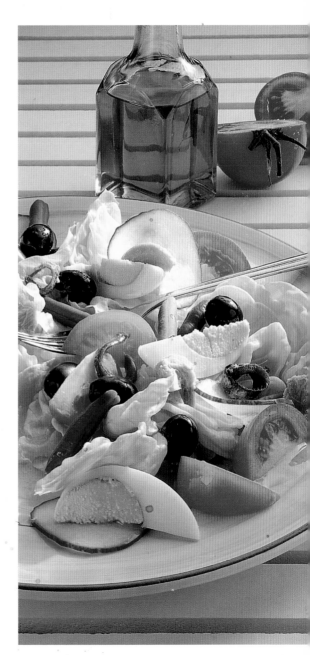

Panzanella

- specialty from Italy
- make ahead

This bread salad from Tuscany is a great way to use up your leftover bread. It is best when served cold or served at room temperature.

Serves 4:
8 oz stale crusty white
** bread, crust removed**
6 tbs olive oil
3 tbs red wine vinegar
2 tbs balsamic vinegar
2 tbs water
1 1/4 lb ripe tomatoes
1 onion
2 cloves garlic
2 tbs capers
Salt & pepper to taste
1 bunch fresh basil

Preparation time: 40 minutes
Per serving: 390 calories
7 g protein / 23 g fat / 41 g
carbohydrates

1 Cut the white bread into finger-width slices, then into cubes. In a nonstick skillet, heat 2 tbs of the olive oil over medium heat. Add the bread cubes and sauté until golden brown on all sides. Transfer the bread to a large bowl. In a small bowl, stir together 1 tbs of the red wine vinegar, the balsamic vinegar, and water. Drizzle the vinegar mixture over the bread, toss well, and let it stand, covered, for 15 minutes.

2 Wash the tomatoes, and remove the stems. Cut the tomatoes into 1/2-inch slices, then into cubes, and place them in another large bowl. Peel and finely chop the onion. Peel and mince the garlic and add it to the bowl with the tomatoes, along with the chopped onion and the capers.

3 In a small bowl, whisk the remaining 2 tbs red wine vinegar, salt, pepper, and the remaining 1/4 cup of the olive oil to make a dressing. Wash and shake dry the basil, chop the basil leaves coarsely, and mix them into the tomato mixture.

4 Add the marinated bread cubes to the bowl with the vegetables, pour the salad dressing over it, and toss well. Let the salad stand briefly. Season with salt and pepper before serving.

GREEK
Farmer's Salad

- easy
- specialty from Greece

Serves 4:
1 cucumber
1 green bell pepper
1 lb ripe tomatoes
1 red onion
8 oz Greek sheep's cheese
4 oz black olives, pitted
1/4 cup white wine vinegar
6 tbs olive oil
Salt & pepper to taste
1 tbs fresh oregano leaves

Preparation time: 25 minutes
Per serving: 430 calories / 11 g
protein/37 g fat/17 g
carbohydrates

1 Peel the cucumber, cut it in half lengthwise, and scrape out the seeds with a spoon. Cut the cucumber into pieces about 1/3-inch wide. Trim and wash the green pepper, and cut it into rings. Wash the tomatoes, and cut each tomato into eight pieces, removing the stems as you cut.

2 Peel the onion, and cut it into half-rings. Put the cucumber, green pepper, tomatoes, and onion in a large bowl. Cut the sheep's cheese into small cubes and add them to the bowl. Add the olives.

3 In a small bowl, whisk together the vinegar, olive oil, salt, and pepper to make a dressing. Stir in the oregano.

4 Pour the dressing over the salad ingredients and toss well.

Serving suggestions:
Serve with sliced white bread and chilled Retsina (Greek white wine).

below: Farmer's Salad
above: Panzanella

Noodle-Vegetable Salad

- sophisticated
- specialty from China

Serves 4:
4 oz glass noodles
8 oz fresh shiitake
  mushrooms
2 tbs canola oil
1 red bell pepper
6 oz bean sprouts
1 bunch fresh cilantro
1 piece fresh ginger (about
  3/4 inch)
3 tbs soy sauce
3 tbs unseasoned rice
  vinegar
3 tbs toasted sesame oil
Pepper to taste

Preparation time: 45 minutes
Per serving: 470 calories
15 g protein / 19 g fat / 72 g
carbohydrates

1 Put the glass noodles in a heatproof bowl, pour a generous amount of boiling water over them, and let them stand for 10 minutes. Drain the noodles well, then cut them into small pieces with kitchen scissors.

2 Trim the mushrooms, removing the stems. Rinse the mushrooms briefly in a colander, shaking it well. Pat the mushrooms dry with paper towels, and cut them into small strips. Heat the oil in a skillet over medium heat, add the mushrooms, and sauté until softened, about 10 minutes; cool.

3 Trim and wash the red pepper, and dice it small. Pour boiling water over the bean sprouts, and let them stand for a few seconds. Refresh the sprouts in ice water and drain well. Wash, shake dry, and finely chop the cilantro. Put the cilantro in a large bowl with the red pepper, sprouts, glass noodles, and shiitake mushrooms.

4 Peel and finely chop the ginger. In a small bowl, whisk together the soy sauce, vinegar, sesame oil, and pepper, to make a dressing. Stir in the ginger. Pour the dressing over the salad ingredients, and toss well.

Gado Gado

- good for guests
- specialty from Indonesia

There are many different variations of this salad, some featuring beans, cauliflower, and white cabbage. Any vegetables should be cooked until tender-crisp before tossing in the zesty peanut dressing.

Serves 4:
1 lb boneless chicken
  breasts
2 tbs peanut oil
Salt & pepper to taste
2 tbs sesame seeds
2 cloves garlic
1 onion
1 piece fresh ginger (about
  the size of a walnut)
2 tbs toasted sesame oil
5 oz peanut butter
1/2 cup coconut milk
Scant 1/2 cup water
Red chile flakes to taste
1 small head Chinese
  cabbage (about 10 oz)
2 carrots

Preparation time: 40 minutes
Per serving: 510 calories
35 g protein / 36 g fat / 16 g
carbohydrates

1 Cut the chicken into narrow strips. In a skillet (do not use nonstick), heat the peanut oil over medium heat. Add the chicken and sauté until cooked through, about 5 minutes. Season the chicken with salt and pepper and remove from the pan. Add the sesame seeds to the skillet, and sauté briefly—just until golden brown—and remove from the heat.

2 Peel and mince the garlic, onion, and ginger. In the skillet, heat the sesame oil over medium heat. Add the ginger, and half of the onion and sauté until the onion is translucent. Add the garlic and sauté briefly. Add the peanut butter, coconut milk, and water, and whisk everything until a creamy sauce forms. Season the sauce with salt, pepper, and chile flakes, and cool.

3 Trim the cabbage, cut it in half lengthwise, and cut it into very narrow strips. Wash and dry the cabbage strips, and place

them in a large bowl. Peel and grate the carrots, then add them to the salad bowl.

4 Add the remaining onion to the bowl and toss well. Distribute the cabbage mixture among 4 serving plates. Distribute the chicken breast over the cabbage, pour the peanut sauce over the top, and sprinkle with the sesame seeds.

Serving suggestion: Hot cooked rice is the perfect companion to this salad, drizzled with some of the peanut sauce.

Variation
Instead of chicken breast, you can use cooked, peeled shrimp.

below: Noodle–Vegetable Salad
above: Gado Gado

Eggplant & Zucchini Salad

● easy
● specialty from Turkey

Serves 4:
2 large red bell peppers
10 oz large tomatoes
1 1/2 lb eggplant
1 lb zucchini
6 tbs olive oil
Salt & pepper to taste
2 tsp sweet paprika
1 tsp ground cumin
3 cloves garlic
6-8 tbs fresh lemon juice
1 bunch fresh mint

Preparation time: 45 minutes
Per serving: 290 calories
5 g protein / 21 g fat / 25 g
carbohydrates

1 Preheat the grill or broiler. Trim and wash the peppers and cut them lengthwise into eighths. Grill or broil the pepper pieces for about 8 minutes (if broiling, place the peppers on a foil-lined pan skin-side up), until the skin blackens and blisters. Let the peppers cool under a kitchen towel.

2 Meanwhile, briefly plunge the tomatoes into boiling water to loosen the skins. With a paring knife, slip off the tomato skins. Cut the tomatoes in half and squeeze out the seeds. Dice the tomatoes. Wash and trim the eggplant and zucchini, and cut them into 1/3-inch cubes.

3 Peel the red pepper strips: Lift up the skin with a sharp knife, and then pull off the skins, starting from the tip. Cut each pepper piece into narrow strips.

4 In a large skillet, heat the olive oil over medium-high heat. Add the eggplant cubes and sauté until softened, about 5 minutes. Add the zucchini cubes, and sauté for another 3 minutes. Season with salt, pepper, paprika, and cumin. Peel and mince the garlic, add it to the skillet, and sauté briefly. Transfer the vegetable mixture to a bowl and stir in the lemon juice.

5 Add the tomatoes and red pepper strips to the skillet and sauté briefly, just to heat through. Add the skillet contents to the other vegetables, mix well, and season to taste.

6 Wash and shake dry the mint, and finely chop the leaves. Mix the mint into the salad and serve lukewarm or cold.

Tabbouleh

● inexpensive
● specialty from the Middle East

This bulgur-vegetable salad is marvelously refreshing, especially on hot days, because of the lemon juice and mint.

Serves 4:
4 oz fine bulgur wheat
1 cup lukewarm water
2 large tomatoes (about 1 lb)
1 cucumber
1 bunch green onions
1 bunch fresh Italian parsley
1 bunch fresh mint
Juice from 3 lemons
Salt & pepper to taste
Pinch of ground cumin
5 tbs olive oil

Preparation time: 55 minutes
Per serving: 270 calories
8 g protein /15 g fat / 33 g
carbohydrates

1 In a medium bowl, mix the bulgur with the water and let stand for 30-60 minutes, until the water is fully absorbed. If necessary, add a little more water.

2 Meanwhile, wash the tomatoes, cut them in half, remove the stems, and squeeze out the seeds. Dice the tomatoes small and put them in a medium bowl. Peel the cucumber, cut it in half lengthwise, and remove the seeds with a spoon. Cut the cucumber into small dice and add to the bowl. Trim and wash the green onions, slice them into thin rings, and add them to the bowl.

3 Wash and shake dry the parsley and mint, and remove the leaves from the stems. Coarsely chop the herb leaves and add them to the bowl, along with the bulgur wheat, and toss well.

4 In a small bowl, whisk together the lemon juice, salt, pepper, cumin, and olive oil to make a dressing. Pour the dressing over the salad, mix well, and let stand, covered, for 15 minutes. Check the seasonings before serving.

Serving suggestion:
Serve with warm pita bread and beer or light-bodied red wine.

below: Eggplant & Zucchini Salad
above: Tabbouleh

Seafood Salad with Vegetables

● specialty from Spain
● make ahead

Serves 4:
1 red bell pepper
1 green bell pepper
1 small cucumber
1 onion
2 large tomatoes
5 tbs olive oil
8 oz sea scallops, side
  muscle removed
6 oz peeled, cooked shrimp
3 tbs sherry vinegar
Salt & pepper to taste
2 cloves garlic
1 bunch fresh Italian
  parsley
Lettuce leaves for serving

Preparation time: 30 minutes
Marinating time: 1 hour
Per serving: 330 calories / 21 g
protein / 20 g fat / 21 g
carbohydrates

1 Wash and trim the red and green peppers. Peel the cucumber, cut it in half lengthwise, and scrape out the seeds with a spoon. Peel the onion. Dice the onion, peppers, and cucumber very small, and put them in a bowl.

2 Briefly plunge the tomatoes into boiling water to loosen the skin. With a paring knife, slip off the tomato skins and cut the tomatoes into small dice. Add the tomatoes to the bowl.

3 In a skillet, heat 1 tbs of the oil over medium heat. Add the scallops and sauté until just cooked through, turning once, about 3 minutes. Let the scallops cool, cut them into small pieces, and add the to bowl with the vegetables along with the shrimp.

4 In a small bowl, whisk together the vinegar, remaining 1/4 cup olive oil, salt, and pepper to make a dressing. Peel and mince the garlic, and mix it into the dressing. Wash and shake dry the parsley, finely chop the leaves, and mix them into the dressing. Pour the dressing over the salad, toss well, cover, and refrigerate for 1 hour to blend the flavors.

5 Wash the lettuce leaves, pat dry, then use them to line a serving platter or 4 serving plates. Spoon the salad on top of the lettuce leaves.

Serving suggestion: Use jumbo, decorative seashells as bases for serving the salad.

Herring Salad with Beets

● easy
● specialty from
   Scandinavia

Serves 4:
1 1/4 lb boiling potatoes
1 lb small beets
2 eggs
1 onion
2 dill pickles
1 tart apple
2–3 tbs fresh lemon juice
8 herring fillets
1 bunch fresh dill
1 cup sour cream
1/4 cup white wine
  vinegar
Salt & pepper to taste

Preparation time: 1 hour
Marinating time: 30 minutes
Per serving: 870 calories
75 g protein / 46 g fat / 36 g
carbohydrates

1 Wash the potatoes and beets. In separate pots of boiling water, cook the potatoes and beets until tender, about 20 and 30 minutes respectively. Drain off the water, and let the vegetables cool. Boil the eggs for about 10 minutes, until the yolks are cooked hard. Plunge the eggs into ice water, let them stand for a few minutes, then peel and rinse the eggs.

2 Peel and finely chop the onion. Finely chop the pickles. Peel the apple, quarter it, and remove the core. Cut the apple into small dice, and drizzle with lemon juice.

3 Peel the potatoes and beets, and cut them into 1/3-inch cubes. Place the cubes in a bowl, along with the onion, pickles, and apple. Cut the herring fillets crosswise into wide strips and add them to the bowl.

4 Wash, shake dry, and finely chop the dill. In a bowl, stir together the sour cream, vinegar, salt, and pepper to make a dressing. Mix in the dill, and pour the dressing over the salad. Toss the salad well, cover, and refrigerate for 30 minutes to blend the flavors.

5 At serving time, cut the hard-boiled eggs into quarters and arrange them on top of the salad.

As a light meal, a salad is ideal—whether for lunch, dinner, or anytime in between. Usually featuring meat, poultry, seafood, cheese, or hearty vegetables, entrée salads are a great way to maintain a light lifestyle. Salad ingredients should be fresh, crisp, and well balanced. Start with the recipes on the following pages. Once you get used to putting them together, you'll be able to create fabulous, filling salads on your own.

About Lettuce

Leaf lettuces are the stars on the salad plate. Due to modern growing practices and transportation systems, most types of lettuce are available year-round.

Arugula: Originally from Italy, this salad green, also called rocket, is developing a following in this country. The dark green, serrated leaves have a peppery flavor.

Belgian endive: The bitter core should always be removed from this white lettuce with light-green tips. To do so, use a small knife to cut the core away from the leaves from the root end. The leaves themselves can be left whole, or cut into strips.

Butter lettuce: This lettuce is so named because of its silky, tender leaves. Somewhat bland in flavor, butter lettuce is a good base for salads with assertive flavors.

Frisée: This frizzy-looking lettuce belongs to the endive family. It has light yellow to dark green, finely feathered leaves. Its flavor is slightly bitter.

Iceberg lettuce: An American original, it's light green, and has crunchy, meaty leaves. Though bland in flavor, iceberg does not get limp as fast as other lettuces, and can therefore be stored for several days.

Leaf lettuce: Available in red or green varieties, heads of this type of lettuce have curly, almost serrated leaves.

Mâche: Also called lamb's lettuce and corn salad, mâche is usually found during the fall and winter

Entrée Salads

months. Mâche grows in little dark-green clusters and has a hearty flavor. Since it grows in sandy soil, take extra care to wash mâche thoroughly.

Oakleaf lettuce: This is a variety of leaf lettuce with red-tipped leaves, which resemble oak leaves in shape.

Radicchio: This comes in compact heads with red to pink-red leaves and white ribs. The flavor is pleasantly bitter. Radicchio is ideal for mixing with other leaf lettuce varieties.

Romaine lettuce: this workhorse green is very versatile, with sturdy, long, dark green leaves. On bigger heads of romaine, it's wise to remove the tough white ribs before cutting or tearing the romaine leaves into pieces.

Mixed Greens

Mesclun is a fancy word for baby mixed salad greens. You can find these mixes loose or in bags at most supermarkets and specialty foods stores. You can even find seeds to grow the mesclun salad mix in your garden, if you're so inclined. Salad mixes are now available with a wide variety of lettuces, garnishes, and in some cases salad dressings. Found in cellophane bags, these are fine if you are in a hurry, but are not recommended for everyday salads. Though most bags say that the greens have been pre-washed, it's wise to wash them again thoroughly before eating.

Preparing Lettuce

• Sort the lettuce and remove any wilted or spoiled parts. Cut off the ribs or tough stems if necessary. Wash the lettuce well in a colander and spin it dry in a salad spinner. If you don't have a salad spinner, pat it dry well with paper towels. Dry lettuce is important, so that the salad dressing will cling to the leaves.

• If desired, prepare more lettuce than you need for the meal and save the surplus for later. To store, pack the lettuce loosely into locking freezer bags. In the vegetable compartment of the refrigerator, the lettuce will stay fresh for 3-4 days.

Adding Crunch to Salads

For many salad eaters, crunch is an important element. Below are suggestions for increasing the sensation.

• Add nuts or seeds to the salad before serving. Choose shelled pumpkin seeds (pepitas), pine nuts, sunflower kernels, peanuts, or almond slivers. For extra flavor and crispness, toast nuts or seeds briefly in a nonstick skillet before sprinkling on the salad.

• Sprinkle the salad with homemade croutons. Cut white bread into cubes, and sauté them until golden brown in olive oil or butter. If desired, you can add minced garlic, minced fresh herbs, or chili powder to taste.

Clockwise from the bottom: pumpkin and sunflower seeds, frisée, Belgian endive, radicchio, butter lettuce, iceberg lettuce, romaine, red leaf lettuce, mâche, arugula, and oakleaf lettuce.

Lamb Meatballs on Leaf Lettuce

● good for guests
◐ easy

Serves 2:
10 oz ground lamb
1 egg
2 tbs ground almonds
2 tbs fine bread crumbs
2 cloves garlic
Salt & pepper to taste
Pinch of cayenne pepper
6 tbs olive oil
1 small head butter
  lettuce
1 small head radicchio
1 shallot
1 tbs sherry vinegar
1 tsp fresh oregano leaves

Preparation time: 30 minutes
per serving: 670 calories
23 g protein / 58 g fat / 15 g
carbohydrates

1 In a bowl, combine the lamb, egg, almonds, and bread crumbs. Peel and mince the garlic. Add half of the garlic to the bowl, and season well with salt, pepper, and cayenne. Mix well with your hands.

2 Preheat the oven to 150°F. With wet hands, form 10-12 small balls from the lamb mixture. In a skillet, heat 2 tbs of the olive oil over medium heat. Add the meatballs and brown on all sides. Remove the meatballs from the pan and keep them warm in the oven.

3 Trim and separate the butter lettuce leaves. Trim the radicchio, and cut it into narrow strips. Wash and dry the lettuces. Peel the shallot and cut it into fine rings.

4 In a large bowl, whisk the vinegar with the remaining 1/4 cup olive oil, salt, pepper, and oregano to make a dressing. Stir in the remaining 1/2 of the minced garlic.

5 Add the lettuce and shallots to the bowl and toss the salad well. Distribute the salad on 2 plates. Arrange the warm meatballs on top.

Warm Vegetable Salad with Ginger

◐ for staying slim
● sophisticated

Serves 2:
8 oz Chinese cabbage
2 small zucchini
1 red bell pepper
6 oz mushrooms
1 piece fresh ginger (about
  1/3 inch)
2 cloves garlic
2 tbs soybean oil
2 tbs toasted sesame oil
1 tsp Chinese 5-spice
  powder
Salt & pepper to taste
2-3 tbs fresh lemon juice
1 tbs soy sauce

Preparation time: 30 minutes
Per serving: 250 calories
5 g protein / 21 g fat / 13 g
carbohydrates

1 Trim the cabbage, cut it in half lengthwise, and slice it finely. Wash and dry the cabbage. Trim and wash the zucchini, and slice it very thinly. Trim and wash the red pepper, and dice it small. Trim and briefly wash the mushrooms, then slice them thinly. Peel and finely chop the ginger and garlic.

2 In a wide saucepan or wok, heat half of the soybean and sesame oils over medium-high heat. Add the mushrooms and sauté until softened, about 5 minutes, then transfer them to a plate. Add the remaining oils to the pan and reduce the heat to medium. Add the cabbage and zucchini and sauté until softened, about 5 minutes. Add the ginger, garlic, and red pepper to the pan and sauté briefly. Return the mushrooms to the pan and sauté to heat through. Season with the 5-spice powder, salt, and pepper.

3 Stir in the lemon juice and soy sauce, bring briefly bring to a boil, then arrange the warm mixture on 2 plates.

Variations

To create a heartier meal:
Add 8 oz peeled, cooked
medium shrimp to the
pan and heat through
just before serving.

Or

Add 8 oz cooked boneless
chicken breast strips to
the pan and heat through
just before serving.

Or

Add 1/4 peeled fresh
pineapple, cut into small
pieces, and heat through
just before serving.

below: Warm Vegetable
Salad with Ginger
above: Lamb Meatballs on
Leaf Lettuce

Steak Strips on Green Leaf Lettuce

● for staying slim
● fast

Serves 2:
1/4 cup canola oil
2 beef fillet steaks (about 6 oz each)
Salt & pepper to taste
1 small head green leaf lettuce
1/2 bunch fresh Italian parsley
1 orange
1 small red onion
2 tbs white wine vinegar

Preparation time: 30 minutes
Per serving: 300 calories
30 g protein / 20 g fat / 8 g carbohydrates

1 In a skillet, heat 1 tbs of the oil over medium heat until very hot; add the steaks and cook for about 6 minutes per side, depending on their thickness, turning once. The meat should still be slightly pink inside. Season the steaks with salt and pepper, remove them from the pan, and cool. Cut the cooled meat into thin slices.

2 Trim the lettuce, tear it into large pieces, then wash and dry it. Wash the parsley, shake dry, and pick off the leaves. With a sharp knife, remove the orange peel and inner white pith to expose the fruit. Cut between the membranes to release the orange segments. Cut the segments in half crosswise. Peel the onion, quarter it, and cut it into thin slices.

3 In a medium bowl, whisk together the vinegar, remaining 3 tbs oil, salt, and pepper to make a dressing. Toss the steak strips in the dressing and remove.

4 Add the parsley, onion, and lettuce to the bowl, toss with the dressing, and distribute the mixture on 2 plates. Arrange the steak strips on top in a fan shape, and garnish with the orange pieces.

Serving suggestions:
Serve with toasted slices of baguette and herb butter, and a California Chardonnay.

Cheese Salad with Garlicky Nuts

◐ easy
● sophisticated

Serves 2:
2 heads Belgian endive
8 oz Emmentaler cheese,
  sliced 1/2-inch thick
1 small red onion
4 oz purple grapes
2 tbs white wine vinegar
3 tbs walnut oil
Salt & pepper to taste
1 clove garlic
1 tbs butter
2 oz walnut halves

Preparation time: 30 minutes
Per serving: 720 calories
33 g protein / 58 g fat / 23 g
carbohydrates

1 Cut the endive in half lengthwise, and remove the bitter core. Separate and set aside 6 pretty leaves; cut the remaining endive into 1/3-inch strips. Wash and dry all of the endive.

2 Cut the cheese in small cubes. Peel and finely dice the onion. Put the onion, cheese, and endive strips in a medium bowl. Wash the grapes, cut them in half, remove the seeds, and add the grapes to the bowl.

3 In a small bowl, whisk together the vinegar, walnut oil, salt, and pepper to make a dressing. Pour the dressing over the salad ingredients and toss well. Arrange the reserved endive leaves on 2 plates, and distribute the salad on top.

4 Peel and mince the garlic. In a skillet, melt the butter over medium heat and add the walnuts. Add the garlic to the pan and sauté briefly, until aromatic. Sprinkle the warm garlicky nuts over the salad and serve.

Variations
You can substitute cubed pears or apples (drizzled with lemon juice to prevent discoloration) for the grapes. White bread cubes, sautéed until golden brown, can stand in for the walnuts.

Shrimp on Snow Peas

● easy
● good for guests

Serves 2:
6 peeled, cooked jumbo
  shrimp
5 tbs lemon juice
Salt to taste
10 oz snow peas
1 ripe avocado
Pepper to taste
1/2 bunch fresh cilantro
Pinch of cayenne pepper
3 tbs white wine vinegar
3 tbs soybean oil

Preparation time: 30 minutes
Per serving: 450 calories
21 g protein / 33 g fat / 21 g
carbohydrates

1 Rinse the shrimp in
cold water, pat dry, and
drizzle with 2 tbs of the
lemon juice.

2 Bring a large pot of
salted water to boil. Trim
the snow peas, and
remove the strings if
necessary. Wash the peas,
then toss them into the
boiling water for 2
minutes. Drain the peas,
immediately plunge them
into ice water, and drain
again well.

3 Peel the avocado, cut it
in half lengthwise, and
remove the pit. Cut one
avocado half into small
dice, and immediately
drizzle it with 2 tbs of the
lemon juice. Season the
diced avocado with salt

and pepper, and place it
in the refrigerator. Cut
the other avocado half
into large pieces, and
place it in a blender or
food processor with the
remaining 1 tbs of the
lemon juice.

4 Rinse and shake dry
the cilantro, remove the
leaves from the stems,
and puree half of the
leaves with the avocado.
Season with salt, pepper,
and cayenne.

5 In a large bowl, whisk
together the vinegar, oil,
salt, and pepper to make
a dressing. Chop the
remaining cilantro leaves
coarsely, and mix them
into the dressing.

6 Add the snow peas and
avocado cubes to the
bowl, toss them with the
dressing, and distribute
on 2 plates. Arrange the
shrimp on top and
garnish each plate with a
dollop of avocado puree.

Chicken Breast on Mixed Greens

● sophisticated
● make ahead

Serves 2:
2 shallots
2 tbs sherry vinegar
2 tbs olive oil
1 tbs honey
Pepper to taste
Pinch of ground cumin
2 boneless chicken breast
  halves
6 oz mesclun (see p 29)
1 tbs soy sauce
1 tsp Dijon-style mustard
3 tbs peanut oil
Salt to taste
2 tbs shelled peanuts

Preparation time: 20 minutes
Marinating time: 30 minutes
per serving: 570 calories
30 g protein / 47 g fat / 9 g
carbohydrates

1 Peel and finely chop
the shallots. In a small
bowl, whisk 1 tbs of the
vinegar with 1 tbs of the
olive oil, and the honey to
make a marinade. Stir in
the shallots, pepper, and
the cumin.

2 Rinse the chicken
breasts with cold water,
and pat dry well. In a
skillet, heat the remaining
2 tbs olive oil over
medium heat. Add the
chicken breasts and cook
for about 10 minutes,
turning once, until they
are cooked through. Cut
the chicken breasts

against the grain into
thin slices, and place
them on a platter. Pour
the marinade evenly over
the chicken breasts, and
let stand, covered, for
30 minutes.

3 Meanwhile, wash and
dry the mesclun.

4 In a medium bowl,
whisk together the
remaining 1 tbs sherry
vinegar, the soy sauce,
mustard, peanut oil, salt,
and pepper to make a
dressing. Coarsely chop
the peanuts, and stir half
of them into the dressing.

5 Add the greens to the
bowl, toss well, and
distribute on 2 plates.
Arrange the chicken
breast on top of the
lettuce, and sprinkle
the remaining peanuts
on top.

below: Shrimp on Snow
Peas
above: Chicken Breast on
Mixed Greens

Mâche with Chicken Livers

● easy
● good for guests

Serves 2:
6 oz mâche
6 oz cherry tomatoes
1 small onion
1 small bunch fresh chives
2 tbs red wine vinegar
5 tbs canola oil
Pinch of sugar
Salt & pepper to taste
10 oz chicken livers
3 tbs port (or grape juice)

Preparation time: 30 minutes
Per serving: 440 calories
20 g protein / 32 g fat / 15 g
carbohydrates

1 Trim the mâche, then wash and dry it thoroughly. Wash the tomatoes, and cut them in half. Peel and finely dice the onion. Rinse and finely chop the chives.

2 In a large bowl, whisk together the vinegar, 3 tbs of the oil, the sugar, salt, and pepper to make a dressing.

3 Remove the skins and sinews from the chicken livers; briefly rinse with cold water, pat dry, and separate them into their natural segments. In a skillet, heat the remaining 2 tbs oil over medium heat. Add the livers and sauté until browned and firm, about 3 minutes.

Season with salt and pepper. Off the heat, add the port to the pan and stir to coat the livers well.

4 Add the mâche, tomatoes, onions, and half of the chives to the bowl with the dressing, toss well, and arrange on 2 plates.

5 Distribute the warm chicken livers on top of the salad, drizzle with the pan drippings, and sprinkle with the remaining chives.

Serving suggestions:
Serve with buttered walnut bread, and a medium-bodied red wine, such as Spanish Rioja.

Mushroom Salad with Peppers and Salami

● fast
● easy

Serves 2:
1 red bell pepper
1 yellow bell pepper
1 onion
8 oz salami, sliced 1/4-inch
  thick
10 oz white mushrooms
1/2 bunch fresh thyme
1/4 cup olive oil
1 clove garlic
2 tbs balsamic vinegar
Salt & pepper to taste
Pinch of cayenne pepper
Lettuce leaves

Preparation time: 25 minutes
Per serving: 440 calories
11 g protein / 38 g fat / 16 g
carbohydrates

1 Cut the peppers lengthwise into eight pieces each, trim and wash them, and cut them crosswise into narrow slices. Peel the onion, cut it into quarters, and slice it finely. Pull off the skin from the salami, if present, and dice it small. Trim the mushrooms, rinse them briefly, and cut them into thick slices. Wash and shake dry the thyme, and pull the leaves from the stalks.

2 In a skillet, heat 1 tbs of the oil over medium heat. Add the salami cubes, then the

mushrooms, and sauté for 5 minutes. Peel and mince the garlic, add it to the skillet along with the thyme leaves, and sauté the mixture briefly.

3 In a medium bowl, whisk together the vinegar, remaining 3 tbs oil, salt, pepper, and cayenne to make a dressing. Add the red and yellow pepper strips and the onions and toss well.

4 Gently toss the warm mushroom-salami mixture with the pepper mixture. Line 2 salad plates with lettuce leaves, and distribute the salad on top.

Serving suggestions:
Serve with sliced farmer's bread and beer.

Fresh Tuna on Radicchio

● easy
● fast

Serves 2:
2 tuna fillets (each about 5 oz)
1 tbs fresh lemon juice
1 head radicchio
1 bunch watercress
2 tbs red wine vinegar
5 tbs olive oil
Salt & pepper to taste
1 tbs sweet mustard
1 tbs tomato puree
2 tbs capers
1 shallot
1 clove garlic

Preparation time: 25 minutes
Per serving: 540 calories
36 g protein / 41 g fat / 6 g
carbohydrates

1 Rinse the tuna with cold water, pat dry, and cut into bite-sized pieces. Place the tuna in a bowl, drizzle with lemon juice, cover, and refrigerate.

2 Separate the radicchio into individual leaves, then wash and dry it. Wash the watercress well, shake dry, and pick off the leaves.

3 In a medium bowl, whisk together the vinegar, 3 tbs of the olive oil, salt, pepper, mustard, and tomato puree to make a dressing. Finely chop the capers. Peel and finely dice the shallot.

Mix the capers and shallot into the dressing.

4 In a skillet, heat the remaining 2 tbs olive oil over medium heat. Add the tuna cubes and sauté for 2-3 minutes. Peel and mince the garlic, add it to the pan, and sauté briefly. Season the mixture with salt and pepper.

5 Gently toss the radicchio and watercress in the dressing, and distribute on 2 plates. Arrange the warm tuna cubes on top.

Serving suggestions:
Serve with baguette slices and herb butter.

Variations
Instead of tuna, other kinds of fish, such as salmon or cod, are equally suitable for this recipe. In a pinch, tuna from a can works as well (you don't need to sauté it).

Oakleaf Lettuce with Warm Goat Cheese Toasts

● good for guests
● sophisticated

Serves 2:
1 small head oakleaf lettuce
2 green onions
1 small apple
1 tbs fresh lemon juice
2 tbs cider vinegar
3 tbs sunflower oil
Salt & pepper to taste
1 tsp honey
1 tbs sunflower kernels
4 slices baguette
1 clove garlic
4 oz soft goat cheese

Preparation time: 25 minutes
Per serving: 640 calories
22 g protein / 41 g fat / 47 g
carbohydrates

1 Preheat the broiler. Trim, wash and dry the lettuce. Trim and wash the green onions, and slice them into fine rings. Wash and dry the apple, cut it into eighths, and remove the core. Dice the apple and drizzle with the lemon juice to prevent discoloration.

2 In a medium bowl, whisk together the cider vinegar, oil, salt, pepper, and honey to make a dressing. Stir in the onion, apple, and sunflower kernels.

3 Toast the baguette slices. Peel the garlic, cut

the clove in half, and rub one side each of the toast slices with the cut side of the garlic. Cut the goat cheese into eight slices, divide them among the toast slices, and place on a foil-lined baking sheet. Place the toasts under the broiler for about 1 minute, until the cheese is bubbly and the bread is slightly browned.

4 Toss the salad in the dressing, distribute it on 2 plates, and place the toasts, fresh from the oven, on top. Grind some fresh pepper over the top, if desired.

below: Oakleaf Lettuce with Warm Goat Cheese Toasts
above: Fresh Tuna on Radicchio

Salad Classics

The most important thing to remember when making salads is that a salad is only as good as its ingredients. If you buy the best quality ingredients—including the vinegar and oil used for the dressing—every salad can become a classic.

Vinegar & Oil

Vinegar
Balsamic vinegar: Known in Italy as *aceto balsamico*—balsamic vinegar comes from Modena. To achieve its proper consistency and flavor, the vinegar is stored for at least 3 years in a succession of barrels made from different types of wood. The longer it is stored, the thicker, more flavorful, and more expensive the vinegar will be.

Balsamic vinegar must mature for a few years in a sequence of wood barrels.

Cider vinegar: Made from fermented apple cider, this vinegar has a balanced, pleasantly sour apple flavor.
Flavored vinegar: A variety of substances can be used to make interesting flavored vinegars, such as herbs, garlic, raspberries, capers, etc. Usually white wine vinegar is used as the base for flavored vinegars.
Sherry vinegar: Particularly aromatic, sherry vinegar is produced from fine Spanish sherry. Used sparingly, its flavor goes a long way.
Wine vinegar: Produced from red or white wine, wine vinegars are versatile ingredients, compliment-ing a wide range of salad ingredients. Champagne vinegar is a delicious, bright variation of white wine vinegar.

Oil
Canola Oil: Pressed from rapeseeds, canola oil is a versatile, neutral oil. Canola has a high content of monounsaturated fats and Omega-3 fatty acids, both of which are known for their health benefits.
Olive oil: Produced all over the Mediterranean region—and now in some parts of North America—olive oil is one of the

most popular oils on the market today. Replete with monounsaturated fats, olive oil is a sensible choice in a health-conscious lifestyle. There are 3 different levels of quality: extra-virgin olive oil, from the first cold pressing; pure olive oil, from subsequent pressings and often refined; and pomace olive oil, made by adding a solvent to the residue left from making the other olive oils. The flavor and character of olive oil varies depending on its level of refinement and its place of origin.

Nut oils: Common types of nut oils are made from hazelnuts, almonds, or peanuts, and often have a very intense flavor. For salad dressings, it's usually best to mix a nut oil with a neutral oil to mellow the flavor.

Pumpkin seed oil: This strongly flavored dark green oil is obtained from hulled pumpkin seeds. It is best used with hearty salads—such as steak salad—or mixed with a more neutral-flavored oil.

Sesame oil: Pressed from sesame seeds, sesame oil comes in 2 varieties. Regular sesame oil is light in color and flavor, and has a mild, nutty flavor. Toasted—or Asian—sesame oil is made from toasted sesame seeds, which creates a more assertive nutty flavor and dark brown color. Toasted sesame oil should be used only sparingly so that it doesn't overwhelm the dish in which it is used.

Soybean oil: Obtained from soybeans, this oil is thought to have the health benefits of soybeans. Soybean oil is a versatile ingredient, due to its neutral flavor and high smoke point.

Sunflower oil: Pressed from sunflower kernels, this oil has similar qualities to soybean oil, with a slightly lower smoke point.

Vegetable oil: Often bottles labeled vegetable oil are a mixture of different plant-based oils. These have a neutral flavor and are very versatile.

Oils should always be stored protected from light and heat in well-closed containers. If you like to use a variety of oils, buy small bottles to prevent them from turning rancid. Opened bottles of most oils should be used within 6 months, nut oils within 3 months. Vinegar keeps for up to 1 year after it is opened.

Start with the best-quality oil and vinegar, and you will create a top-quality salad dressing.

Celery Root Salad with Mustard Dressing

● sophisticated
● easy

Serves 4:
2 very fresh egg yolks, or
   1/4 cup frozen
   pasteurized egg yolks
1 tsp mustard
1 cup canola oil
3 tbs sour cream
2 tbs lemon juice
Salt & pepper to taste
Pinch of sugar
1 celery root (about
   1 1/4 lb)
8 oz celery stalks with
   leaves
1 onion
1 apple
2 oz walnut halves

Preparation time: 30 minutes
Per serving: 450 calories
4 g protein / 53 g fat / 16 g
carbohydrates

1   In a bowl, whisk together the egg yolks and mustard. While whisking, slowly add the oil in a thin stream, until a thick, creamy mixture forms. Stir in the sour cream and 1 tbs of the lemon juice, and season the dressing with salt, pepper, and sugar.

2   Peel the celery root well, then wash, pat dry, and cut into pieces. With a food processor or box grater (using the large holes), grate the celery root into a bowl. Trim and wash the celery stalks, remove the leaves, and cut the stalks into thin slices. Finely chop the celery leaves and add both to the bowl with the celery root.

3   Peel and finely chop the onion. Peel the apple, cut it into eighths, remove the core, and drizzle with the remaining 1 tbs lemon juice. Cut the apple into thin strips, and add them to the bowl along with the onion.

4   Pour the dressing over the salad, toss well, and season to taste. Coarsely chop the walnuts, sprinkle them over the salad, and serve.

Tomato-Mozzarella Salad

● make ahead
● fast

Serves 4:
1 1/2 lb ripe tomatoes
2 shallots
6 oz mozzarella cheese
4 oz black olives, pitted
1/4 cup red wine vinegar
5 tbs olive oil
Salt & pepper to taste
2 cloves garlic
1 bunch fresh basil

Preparation time: 25 minutes
Per serving: 340 calories
10 g protein / 29 g fat / 14 g
carbohydrates

1   Wash the tomatoes, cut them from stem to end into eight pieces, and remove the stems. Place the tomato pieces in a large bowl.

2   Peel and finely chop the shallots. Cut the mozzarella into 1/4-inch slices, then into cubes. Add both, along with the olives, to the bowl with the tomatoes.

3   In a small bowl, whisk together the vinegar, olive oil, salt, and pepper to make a dressing. Peel and mince the garlic, and mix it into the dressing.

4   Pour the dressing over the salad, toss well, and let stand for 10 minutes to blend the flavors.

5   Meanwhile, wash and shake dry the basil, cut larger leaves into thin strips, and keep smaller leaves whole. Mix the basil strips into the salad. Before serving, garnish the salad with the whole basil leaves.

below: Tomato-Mozzarella
Salad
above: Celery Root Salad
with Mustard Dressing

Green Beans, Arugula, & Cherry Tomatoes

● for staying slim
● good for guests

Serves 4:
1 lb green beans
Salt to taste
8 oz cherry tomatoes
1 bunch arugula
1 red onion
3 tbs balsamic vinegar
1/4 cup olive oil
Pepper to taste
1 small clove garlic
2 tbs pine nuts

Preparation time: 45 minutes
Per serving: 200 calories
3 g protein / 16 g fat / 16 g
carbohydrates

1 Trim the beans and remove the strings if necessary. Wash the beans and cut large ones in half. Plunge the beans into a large pot of boiling salted water and cook until tender-crisp, about 10 minutes. Drain the beans and immediately plunge them into ice water to cool. Drain them well.

2 Wash the tomatoes and cut them in half, removing the stems. Put the tomatoes in a large bowl along with the green beans.

3 Pinch the stems off the arugula. Wash and spin dry the arugula leaves, and cut them into fairly wide strips. Peel the onion, cut it into quarters lengthwise, then slice. Add the onion and arugula to the bowl.

4 In a small bowl, stir together the vinegar, olive oil, salt, and pepper to make a dressing. Peel and mince the garlic and stir it into the dressing. Pour the dressing over the salad and toss gently.

5 Toast the pine nuts in a dry nonstick skillet, stirring constantly, until golden brown; sprinkle them over the salad before serving.

Variations

For a more substantial salad, replace the pine nuts with 6 oz salami, diced small. Or, serve the salad as an appetizer for 6 people, and add 3 thin slices of prosciutto to each serving.

Chicken Salad with Pineapple & Sprouts

● sophisticated
● make ahead

Serves 4:
1 1/4 lb boneless chicken
  breasts
2 tbs canola oil
Salt & pepper to taste
1 small fresh pineapple
6 oz soybean sprouts
Handful of fresh chervil
1/2 cup mayonnaise
3 tbs plain yogurt
2–3 tbs fresh lemon juice
Pinch of cayenne pepper
1 tsp Chinese 5-spice
  powder
Pinch of sugar
Lettuce leaves

Preparation time: 45 minutes
Per serving: 550 calories
34 g protein / 37 g fat / 25 g
carbohydrates

1 Rinse the chicken, pat dry, and cut into 1/3-inch strips. In a skillet, heat the oil over medium heat. Add the chicken strips and sauté until cooked through, about 5-10 minutes. Season the chicken with salt and pepper, and cool.

2 Meanwhile, peel the pineapple well, removing the "eyes," quarter it, and cut out the woody core. Cut the pineapple into cubes, and put them in a large bowl.

3 Pour boiling water over the bean sprouts, and let them stand for a few seconds. Refresh the sprouts in ice water and drain well. Cut the chicken into cubes, and add them, along with the sprouts, to the bowl.

4 Wash and shake dry the chervil. Finely chop 2/3 of the leaves; set aside the rest.

5 In a small bowl, stir together the mayonnaise, yogurt, lemon juice, salt, pepper, cayenne, 5-spice powder, and sugar to make a dressing. Stir in the chopped chervil. Pour the dressing over the salad, and mix well.

6 Line a platter with lettuce leaves, and arrange the chicken salad on top. Sprinkle with the remaining chervil leaves.

Cucumber Salad with Dill

● inexpensive
● fast

Serves 4:
1 large cucumber
1/2 bunch fresh dill
1 onion
2/3 cup sour cream
2 tbs walnut oil
3 tbs white wine vinegar
Salt & pepper to taste
Pinch of sugar
2 oz walnut halves

Preparation time: 15 minutes
Per serving: 190 calories
4 g protein / 17 g fat / 10 g
carbohydrates

1 Peel or wash the cucumber, as desired. Slice the cucumber thinly, and put it in a bowl.

2 Rinse and shake dry the dill, then finely chop.

Peel and chop the onion, and add it to the bowl along with the dill.

3 In a small bowl, mix the sour cream with the walnut oil, vinegar, salt, pepper, and sugar to make a dressing. Pour the dressing over the salad and mix well.

4 Just before serving, coarsely chop the walnuts, and sprinkle them over the salad.

> **Tip!** To make an elegant hors d'oeuvre salad, replace the walnuts with 8 oz smoked salmon, cut into strips. Mix the salmon into the salad, or arrange it on top.

Cucumber Salad with Strawberries

● sophisticated
● for staying slender

Serves 4:
1 large cucumber
1 small bunch fresh mint
8 oz fresh strawberries
3 tbs sunflower oil
4–5 tbs lemon juice
2 tsp honey
Salt & pepper to taste
Pinch of cayenne pepper

Preparation time: 20 minutes
Per serving: 130 calories
4 g protein / 11 g fat / 10 g
carbohydrates

1 Peel the cucumber, cut it in half lengthwise, and scrape out the seeds with a spoon. Cut the cucumber halves into slices. Wash and shake dry the mint; keep small

leaves whole, and cut large leaves into strips.

2 Trim and wash the strawberries, and cut them into halves or quarters, depending on size. Put the strawberries and cucumbers in a large salad bowl.

3 In a small bowl, whisk together the oil, lemon juice and honey to make a dressing. Season well with salt, pepper, and cayenne.

4 Sprinkle the chopped mint into the dressing. Add the dressing to the salad and mix well. Let the salad stand briefly to blend the flavors. Garnish the salad with the remaining mint leaves before serving.

Cucumber Salad with Smoked Trout

● good for guests
● make ahead

Serves 4:
1 large cucumber
8 oz tomatoes
1/2 bunch green onions
3 tbs herb vinegar
1/4 cup canola oil
1 tbs tomato puree
Salt & pepper to taste
8 oz smoked trout fillet

Preparation time: 20 minutes
Per serving: 250 calories
15 g protein / 18 g fat / 9 g
carbohydrates

1 Peel the cucumber, cut it in half lengthwise, and scrape out the seeds with a spoon. Cut the cucumber halves into slices, and place them in a large bowl.

2 Wash the tomatoes and cut them each into eight pieces, removing the stems. Trim and wash the green onions, and slice them into thin rings. Add them, along with the tomatoes, to the bowl with the cucumbers.

3 In a small bowl, whisk together the vinegar, oil, tomato puree, salt, and pepper to make a dressing. Pour the dressing over the salad, mix well, and let the salad stand briefly to blend the flavors.

4 Break the trout fillet into pieces, and gently stir them into the salad just before serving.

Cucumber Salad with Sesame and Sprouts

● fast
● easy

Serves 4:
1 cucumber
8 oz carrots
1 pint spicy sprouts, such
  as radish sprouts
2/3 cup plain yogurt
2 tbs toasted sesame oil
3-4 tbs lemon juice
1 clove garlic
1 tsp ground cumin
Salt & pepper to taste
3 tbs sesame seeds

Preparation time: 25 minutes
Per serving: 170 calories
5 g protein / 12 g fat / 12 g
carbohydrates

1 Wash the cucumber, then cut it into small pieces. Put the cucumber in a large bowl.

2 Peel the carrots, coarsely grate them, and add them to the bowl. Rinse the sprouts, shake them dry, and add them to the bowl.

3 In a small bowl, stir together the yogurt, sesame oil, and lemon juice to taste to make a dressing. Peel and mince the garlic, and stir it into the dressing. Season the dressing with the cumin, salt, and pepper, mix well, and pour it over the salad ingredients. Toss the salad well, and let it stand for about 10 minutes to blend the flavors.

4 Toast the sesame seeds in a dry nonstick skillet.. Sprinkle the sesame seeds over the salad.

Butter Lettuce with Radish Sprouts

● easy
● fast

Serves 4:
1 head butter lettuce
2 oz radish sprouts
1 bunch fresh chives
2 tbs sherry vinegar
1/4 cup sunflower oil
1 tsp sweet mustard
Salt & pepper to taste

Preparation time: 15 minutes
Per serving: 140 calories
2 g protein / 14 g fat / 4 g
carbohydrates

1 Trim the lettuce, separate the individual leaves, wash them thoroughly, and spin dry. Tear the large leaves into smaller pieces.

2 Rinse the sprouts well and drain. Wash the fresh chives and finely chop.

3 In a small bowl, whisk together the vinegar, oil, mustard, salt, and pepper to make a dressing. Stir in the chives. Add the dressing to the salad and toss well.

Variations
All kinds of leaf lettuce can be prepared this way, including mesclun or other mixed lettuces.
Mix 4 oz of crumbled blue cheese and 3 tbs crème fraîche into the dressing, reducing the amounts of oil and vinegar by half.

German-Style Potato Salad

● make ahead
● inexpensive

Serves 4:
2 1/4 lb boiling potatoes
2 tsp caraway seeds
1 cup vegetable stock
6 tbs white wine vinegar
Salt & pepper to taste
1 bunch green onions
1 tbs Dijon-style mustard
6 tbs canola oil

Preparation time: 1 hour
Marinating time: 30 minutes
Per serving: 350 calories
6 g protein / 21 g fat / 36 g
carbohydrates

1 Scrub the potatoes well. Put the potatoes in a pot with the caraway seeds and just barely cover with water. Bring the water to a boil, reduce the heat to low,

and simmer, covered, until tender, about 25-30 minutes. Drain the potatoes, and let them cool slightly. With a paring knife, remove the peels from the potatoes, slice them thinly, and put them in a large bowl.

2 In a saucepan, bring the vegetable stock and 3 tbs of the vinegar to a boil. Season the liquid with salt and pepper. Pour the stock mixture over the warm potatoes, and mix gently, trying to prevent the potato slices from breaking. Let the salad stand, covered, for 30 minutes.

3 Meanwhile trim and wash the green onions, slice them into very fine rings, and add all but 2 tbs to the potatoes.

4 In a small bowl, whisk together the remaining 3 tbs vinegar, the mustard, salt, pepper, and oil to make a dressing. Pour the dressing over the potatoes, and mix gently. Season to taste and sprinkle the remaining green onions on top.

Variations

To make the potato salad more substantial, add 4 oz of bacon, fried until crisp and crumbled.

You can also vary the salad in new ways by mixing in one of the following ingredients:

1 bunch radishes, thinly sliced

or

1 cucumber, thinly sliced

or

3 dill pickles, chopped

or

3 tart apples, cubed

below: German-Style Potato Salad
above: Butter Lettuce with Radish Sprouts

Salads are well suited to serving at parties, as they can easily be prepared ahead of time.

Salad Buffet

For a buffet, choose salads that can remain at room temperature for a while and still look and taste appetizing. To keep them looking fresh, mix chopped fresh herbs into the salad shortly before your guests arrive. If you plan to offer leaf lettuce salads on the buffet, don't dress them ahead of time. Instead, place a dish of the dressing and a serving spoon next to the salad and let your guests spoon on their own dressing. Choose salad servers with long handles so that they don't slip into the bowl during the party, causing your guests' hands to get dirty. Offer a large basket with a variety of breads and crackers or breadsticks as an accompaniment to the salad.

Fresh Ingredients

Garlic: Make sure you always buy fresh garlic. If you find a green center in the garlic clove, remove it, as it has an unpleasant bitter flavor.
Fresh herbs: These can be the perfect finishing touch for your homemade salads. Herbs

Party Salads

are best fresh, or, better yet, snipped as needed from your garden.

Onions: For salads, choose onions that are on the sweet side, such as red onions, Maui or Vidalia onions, and shallots. Green onions are also a nice addition.

Flatbread

A great companion to salads is this easy homemade flatbread. Sift 1 1/3 cups of all-purpose flour into a bowl and make a well in the middle. Sprinkle a pinch of salt into the well, add 1 tbs olive oil, and mix it with a little flour to form a paste. A little at a time, kneed in about 1/2 cup lukewarm water and 2 tbs grated Parmesan cheese, until a smooth dough forms (you may not need to use all of the water). Cover the bowl with a towel or plastic wrap, and let the dough rest for 15 minutes. Preheat the oven to 400°F.

Divide the dough into 10 pieces, and, on a floured surface, roll or press each piece into a flat disk about 2 1/2 inches in diameter. Line a baking sheet with parchment paper, place the disks on it, and sprinkle with your choice of toppings: chopped green olives, sesame seeds, caraway seeds, poppy seeds, or coarse sea salt. Bake the breads on the middle oven rack for 10 minutes, until they are puffed and lightly browned.

Homemade flatbread is a good companion to fresh salads.

Fresh herbs are a super addition to salads. From left: mint, thyme, basil, and rosemary

Turkey Salad with Leeks and Oyster Mushrooms

● sophisticated
● for staying slim

Serves 6–8:
Salt to taste
1 1/2 lb leeks
1 lb oyster mushrooms
1 lb boneless turkey breast
6 tbs canola oil
Pepper to taste
1 large red bell pepper
4–5 tbs fresh lemon juice
Pinch of sugar

Preparation time: 35 minutes
Per serving (8): 220 calories
14 g protein / 14 g fat / 10 g
carbohydrates

1 Bring a large pot of salted water to a boil. Trim the leeks, cut them in half lengthwise, and wash them thoroughly. Slice the leeks diagonally into half-rings about 1/4-inch wide. Boil the leeks for 2 minutes, drain, and immediately plunge them into ice water to stop the cooking. Drain the leeks well.

2 Trim the oyster mushrooms, and if necessary, briefly rinse them and pat dry. Slice the mushrooms into 1/3-inch strips.

3 Rinse and pat dry the turkey, cut it into strips, then into bite-sized pieces. In a skillet, heat 2 tbs of the oil over medium-high heat. Add the turkey and sauté until cooked through, about 3–4 minutes. Season the turkey with salt and pepper, remove it from the pan, and cool.

4 Add 1 tbs of the oil to the pan, add the mushrooms, and sauté until softened, about 7 minutes. Season the mushrooms with salt and pepper, remove them from the pan, and cool. Trim and wash the red pepper, and dice it small.

5 In a large bowl, whisk together the lemon juice, salt, pepper, sugar, and the remaining 3 tbs oil to make a dressing. Add the leeks, mushrooms, turkey, and bell pepper to the bowl, and toss well.

Green Pasta Salad with Parmesan Dressing

● to make ahead
◐ easy

Serves 6–8:
Salt to taste
8 oz spinach fettuccine
1 lb broccoli
10 oz frozen peas, thawed
1 lb small zucchini
1 onion
1 bunch fresh chives
1 bunch fresh Italian
  parsley
1 bunch fresh basil
2 cloves garlic
7 tbs olive oil
5 tbs balsamic vinegar
Pepper to taste
2 oz Parmesan cheese,
  freshly grated

Preparation time: 40 minutes
Marinating time: 30 minutes
Per serving (8): 330 calories
14 g protein / 16 g fat / 37 g
carbohydrates

1 Bring a large pot of salted water to a boil, and cook the pasta in it according to the instructions on the package, until slightly firm to the bite (*al dente*). Drain the pasta, collecting the water in a pot. Rinse the pasta with cold water and drain well.

2 Meanwhile, wash the broccoli and separate it into florets. Peel the broccoli stalks and chop them small. Bring the pasta cooking water to a boil, add the broccoli florets and stalks, and cook until tender-crisp, about 6 minutes. Add the peas for the last 3 minutes of cooking. Drain the vegetables, immediately plunge them into ice water, and drain again well.

3 Wash and trim the zucchini, and grate them coarsely. Peel and finely dice the onion. Put both, along with the pasta, broccoli, and peas in a large bowl.

4 Wash, shake dry, and chop the herbs. Peel and mince the garlic. Add both to the salad.

5 In a small bowl, stir together the olive oil, vinegar, salt, pepper, and Parmesan to make a dressing. Pour the dressing over the salad, mix well, and let stand for 30 minutes to blend the flavors before serving.

Tip! Jazz up the salad by mixing in strips of prosciutto to taste.

Sausage Salad with Radishes

● easy
● specialty from Bavaria

Serves 6-8:
1 onion
2 bunches radishes
4-5 dill pickles
2 bunch fresh chives
2 1/4 lb cooked pork
  sausages
5 tbs cider vinegar
6 tbs sunflower oil
Salt & pepper to taste
2 tsp sweet grainy mustard

Preparation time: 30 minutes
Per serving (8): 650 calories
16 g protein / 61 g fat / 9 g
carbohydrates

1 Peel the onion, quarter it, and slice it finely. Trim, wash, and slice the radishes. Slice the pickles. Put the onion, radishes, and pickles in a large bowl. Wash, shake dry, and finely chop the chives, and add them to the bowl.

2 Remove the skin from the sausage, cut the sausage into slices, and add them to the bowl.

3 In a small bowl, whisk together the vinegar, oil, salt, pepper, and mustard to make a dressing, and pour it over the salad. Mix the salad well, cover the bowl, and let it stand briefly to blend the flavors. Season to taste.

Serving suggestion: In Bavarian style, serve with sliced farmer's bread and German beer.

Hearty Lentil Salad

● inexpensive
● make ahead

Serves 6-8:
1 lb French green lentils
1 large onion
2 bay leaves
2 whole cloves
Salt to taste
10 oz bacon, sliced fairly
  thick
6 tbs red wine vinegar
8 oz carrots
1 red bell pepper
1 yellow bell pepper
1 bunch green onions
7 tbs pumpkin seed oil or
  olive oil
2 tsp Dijon-style mustard
Pepper to taste
Pinch of sugar

Preparation time: 1 hour
Soaking time: 12 hours
Per serving (8): 570 calories
30 g protein / 31 g fat / 44 g
carbohydrates

1 Place the lentils in a pot and cover with cold water. Cover the pot and soak the lentils overnight. If necessary, add a little more water to keep the lentils submerged.

2 The next day, peel the onion. Stick the bay leaves and cloves into the onion and add it to the pot with the lentils.

3 Bring the lentils to a boil in the soaking water with 2 tsp salt. Reduce the heat to low and simmer the lentils, covered, until tender, 30-40 minutes. Transfer the lentils to a large bowl. Remove the onion, bay leaves, and cloves.

4 Dice the bacon small. Put the bacon in a nonstick skillet and fry over medium heat until crisp. Pour the bacon, with its fat, into the bowl with the lentils. Mix in 3 tbs of the vinegar.

5 Peel the carrots and coarsely grate them into the bowl. Trim, wash, and cut the red and yellow peppers into small dice. Trim and wash the green onions, slice them finely, and add them, along with the peppers, to the bowl.

6 In a small bowl, whisk together the remaining 3 tbs vinegar, the oil, mustard, salt, pepper, and sugar to make a dressing. Pour the dressing over the lentils and mix well. Allow the salad to stand, covered, for 20 minutes to blend the flavors. Season to taste.

Tip! You can mix smoked sausage with the lentils instead of the bacon. If you are in a hurry, you can use canned lentils; drain them well, and follow the recipe.

below: Hearty Lentil Salad
above: Sausage Salad with Radishes

Vegetable Salad with Mortadella

● fast
◉ easy

Serves 6–8:
2 bulbs fennel
10 oz carrots
2 large red bell peppers
10 oz zucchini
8 oz celery stalks
1 cucumber
10 oz mortadella, thinly sliced
8 oz Gorgonzola cheese, crumbled
2/3 cup crème fraîche
2 tbs canola oil
6–7 tbs lemon juice
Salt & pepper to taste

Preparation time: 30 minutes
Per serving (8): 340 calories
12 g protein / 25 g fat / 17 g carbohydrates

1 Trim the fennel, setting aside the dark green fronds. Cut the bulbs in half, and slice the halves finely. Peel the carrots, and cut them into matchstick-sized strips. Trim and wash the peppers, and cut them lengthwise into thin strips. Trim and wash the zucchini, and cut them into diagonal slices. Trim and wash the celery stalks, and cut them into sticks about 2 inches long; slice any wide stalks in half lengthwise. Peel and slice the cucumber.

2 Cut the mortadella into thin strips. Arrange the vegetables next to one another, along with the mortadella, on a serving platter.

3 In a blender or food processor, puree the Gorgonzola with the crème fraîche, oil, and lemon juice to make a dressing. Season with salt and pepper. Chop the fennel fronds finely, and mix them into the dressing. Serve the dressing separately, so that everyone can mix his or her own salad to taste.

Serving suggestions: Serve with grissini (breadsticks), Italian bread, and an Italian red wine, such as Chianti.

> **Tip!** Mortadella is something like Italian-style baloney. Look for it in specialty food stores or Italian delis. Or, substitute another favorite type of cured meat or sausage.

Egg Salad with Corn

● make ahead
◉ inexpensive

Serves 6–8:
10 eggs
2 cans corn kernels (11 oz each)
2 red bell peppers
1 onion
2 bunches fresh Italian parsley
2/3 cup mayonnaise
1/4 cup plain yogurt
2 tbs curry powder
4–5 tbs lemon juice
Salt & pepper to taste
Pinch of sugar

Preparation time: 40 minutes
Per serving (8): 310 calories
12 g protein / 22 g fat / 20 g carbohydrates

1 Boil the eggs for about 10 minutes, until the yolks are cooked hard. Plunge the eggs into ice water, let them stand for a few minutes, then peel and rinse. With an egg slicer, slice the eggs once lengthwise, and once crosswise, to make tiny cubes. Put the egg cubes in a large bowl.

2 Drain the corn well. Cut the red peppers in half; trim, wash, and dice them small. Peel and finely chop the onion. Wash and shake dry the parsley. Pull the parsley leaves from the stalks and chop them finely. Add the corn, peppers, onion, and parsley to the bowl with the eggs.

3 In a bowl, stir together the mayonnaise, yogurt, curry powder, lemon juice, salt, pepper, and sugar to make a dressing. Pour the dressing over the salad. Mix the salad well, and let it stand, covered, for 15 minutes to blend the flavors.

Serving suggestions: This goes well with warm sesame flatbread (p 51).

> **Tip!** Instead of corn, you can use fresh or frozen peas, which must be blanched (briefly cooked) before mixing into the salad.

below: Egg Salad with Corn
above: Vegetable Salad with Mortadella

Rice Salad with Tuna and Tomatoes

● make ahead
◐ inexpensive

Serves 6–8:
Salt to taste
1 cup long-grain rice
1 cucumber
1 lb large tomatoes
2 cans water-packed tuna
   (6 oz each)
2 bunches fresh Italian
   parsley
5–7 tbs red wine vinegar
7 tbs olive oil
Pepper to taste
2 cloves garlic
4 oz black olives, pitted

Preparation time: 40 minutes
Marinating time: 30 minutes
Per serving (8): 350 calories
17 g protein / 15 g fat / 41 g
carbohydrates

1 Bring a large pot of salted water to a boil. Pour in the rice, as if it were pasta, reduce the heat to low, cover the pan, and let the rice barely simmer for 20 minutes. Drain the rice through a colander, rinse with ice water, drain well, and cool.

2 Meanwhile, peel the cucumber, dice it small, and put it in a large bowl. Plunge the tomatoes into boiling water to loosen the skins. With a paring knife, remove the tomato skins. Cut the tomatoes in half, remove the stems, and squeeze out the seeds. Dice the tomatoes finely, and add them to the bowl.

3 Drain the tuna, and pull it into small pieces with your hands. Put the tuna and rice in the bowl with the vegetables. Wash and shake dry the parsley, pull the leaves off the stems, chop the leaves finely, and sprinkle on top of the salad.

4 In a small bowl, whisk together the vinegar to taste, the olive oil, salt, and pepper to make a dressing. Peel and mince the garlic, and stir it into the dressing.

5 Pour the dressing over the salad ingredients, add the olives, and mix well. Cover the bowl and let the salad stand for 30 minutes to blend the flavors. Season to taste.

Iceberg Lettuce with Smoked Pork

- fast
- easy

Serves 6-8:
1 head iceberg lettuce
  (about 1 1/4 lb)
2 red onions
1 lb boneless smoked pork
2 cloves garlic
5 slices light rye bread
3 tbs butter
6 oz cream cheese,
  softened
3 tbs water
5 tbs cider vinegar
3 tbs canola oil
Salt & pepper to taste
1 tsp sweet paprika
1 bunch fresh Italian
  parsley

Preparation time: 30 minutes
Per serving (8): 300 calories
14 g protein / 18 g fat / 21 g
carbohydrates

1 Trim, wash, and dry the lettuce. Tear the lettuce into bite-sized pieces. Peel and finely chop the onions. Put the onions and lettuce in a bowl. Dice the pork and add it to the bowl.

2 Peel and mince the garlic. Remove the crust from the bread, and cut it into small dice. In a skillet, melt the butter over medium heat. Add the bread cubes and fry until golden brown. Just before the cubes are done, stir in the garlic.

3 In a small bowl, stir together the cream cheese, water, vinegar, and oil to make a dressing. Season with salt, pepper, and paprika. Wash and shake dry the parsley, finely chop the leaves, and mix them into the dressing. Pour the dressing over the salad ingredients and toss well. Before serving, mix in the garlic croutons, or sprinkle them on top.

Tip! If you put the salad on a buffet, it is better to serve the salad, the dressing, and the croutons separately, so that the lettuce and the croutons stay crisp longer.

Potato-Vegetable Salad

● easy
● inexpensive

Serves 8-10:
2 lb boiling potatoes
6 tbs white wine vinegar
Salt & pepper to taste
8 oz carrots
1 cucumber
8 oz celery stalks
1 bunch green onions
3 very fresh egg yolks, or
  6 tbs frozen pasteurized
  egg yolks
1 tbs Dijon-style mustard
2 tbs fresh lemon juice
2 cloves garlic
1 cup canola oil

Preparation time: 1 1/4 hours
Marinating time: 30 minutes
Per serving (10): 290 calories
3 g protein / 25 g fat / 16 g
carbohydrates

1 Wash the potatoes and put them in a pot. Barely cover the potatoes with water and bring the water to a boil. Reduce the heat to low and simmer the potatoes until tender, about 20-30 minutes. Peel the potatoes, let them cool, and cut them into 1/3-inch dice. Put the potatoes in a large bowl. Add the vinegar, salt, and pepper to the bowl and toss the ingredients well. Let the mixture stand for a while to blend all of the flavors.

2 Peel the carrots and cucumber, and dice them

both small. Trim and wash the celery stalks, and slice them thinly. Trim and wash the green onions, and slice them thinly. Add the cucumber, celery, and green onions to the bowl with the potatoes and mix well.

3 In a small bowl, whisk together the egg yolks, salt, pepper, mustard, and lemon juice. Peel and mince the garlic, and stir it in. While whisking, add the oil in a thin stream until the mixture resembles mayonnaise. Season to taste.

4 Add the mayonnaise to the bowl and mix well. Cover the bowl and refrigerate the salad for 30 minutes to blend the flavors before serving.

> **Tip!** You can mix in cubed salami, ham, smoked turkey, or smoked chicken if desired. You can also dress the salad with 1-1 1/2 cups purchased mayonnaise instead of using homemade.

Two-Bean Salad with Avocado Dressing

● sophisticated
● make ahead

Serves 6-8:
1 1/4 lb bacon
1 1/4 lb green beans
Salt to taste
2 onions
3 cans kidney beans
  (15 oz each)
1 large ripe avocado
2-3 cloves garlic
1 bunch arugula
5 tbs olive oil
1/2 cup fresh lemon juice,
  or more to taste
Pepper to taste
Pinch of cayenne pepper

Preparation time: 45 minutes
Marinating time: 30 minutes
Per serving: 300 calories
20 g protein / 20 g fat / 9 g
carbohydrates

1 Cut the bacon into bite-sized pieces. In a nonstick skillet, fry the bacon until crisp, and drain on paper towels.

2 Trim the green beans, removing the strings if necessary, and wash. Bring a large pot of salted water to a boil. Add the beans and simmer them until tender-crisp, about 15 minutes. Drain the beans, then plunge them into ice water to stop the cooking. Drain the beans well, and cut them into 1/3-inch pieces.

3 Peel and finely chop the onions. Put the onions and green beans in a large bowl. Drain the kidney beans well. Add the kidney beans and bacon to the bowl.

4 Peel the avocado, cut it in half, and remove the pit. Cut the avocado into large pieces. Peel the garlic. Put the avocado and garlic in a blender or food processor.

5 Wash the arugula and remove the stems. Add the arugula to the blender or food processor with the olive oil, and lemon juice and puree until smooth. Season the dressing generously with salt, pepper, and cayenne.

6 Pour the dressing over the salad ingredients, mix well, and let stand for at least 30 minutes. Check the seasonings once more before serving.

Serving suggestion:
Warmed whole-wheat tortillas are great as a side dish. To drink, serve Mexican beer.

Tip! Avocados should be used only when they are very ripe, when they gain their creamy consistency and typical flavor. To hasten ripening, wrap unripe avocados in newspaper, and let them stand at room temperature for 2-5 days. Use ripe avocados as soon as possible, or store ripe avocados briefly in the refrigerator.

below: Potato-Vegetable Salad
above: Two-Bean Salad with Avocado Dressing

Credits

Published originally under the title Salate, ©1997
Gräfe und Unzer Verlag GmbH, Munich
English translation for the U.S. market ©2000,
Silverback Books, Inc.

Editor: Jennifer Newens, CCP
Translator: Gerda Dinwiddie
Design and Production: Shanti Nelson
Design: Heinz Kraxenberger
Production: Helmut Giersberg
Photos: Odette Teubner; Aigner Impuls (p 40)

ISBN: 1-930603-45-2

Printed in Hong Kong
through Global Interprint,
Santa Rosa, California, USA

Cornelia Adam
Adam originally worked in the hotel and catering
business, during which time she traveled to many
foreign countries. Later she was able to utilize these
various job-related experiences as editor of a well-
known German women's magazine. Currently she
works as a freelance food journalist and cook-
book author.

Odette Teubner
Teubner grew up among cameras, flood lights, and
experimental kitchens. She received her education
from her father, the internationally known food
photographer Christian Teubner. After a brief
excursion into the field of fashion, she returned to the
field of food, and has since had the rare fortune to
combine profession and hobby.